Wild Horses

Kate Riggs

CREATIVE EDUCATION
CREATIVE PAPERBACKS

Published by Creative Education and Creative Paperbacks
P.O. Box 227, Mankato, Minnesota 56002
Creative Education and Creative Paperbacks
are imprints of The Creative Company
www.thecreativecompany.us

Design by Ellen Huber; production by Joe Kahnke
Art direction by Rita Marshall
Printed in China

Photographs by Alamy (Mark J. Barrett), Corbis (Frans Lanting),
Dreamstime (Arvacsaba, David Burke, Isabel Poulin), iStockphoto
(Lucasdm, through-my-lens), Minden Pictures (Klein and Hubert,
Carol Walker), National Geographic Creative (YVA MOMATIUK
& JOHN EASTCOTT/MINDEN PICTURES), Newscom (Danita
Delimont Photography), Shutterstock (mariait, Anastasija Popova,
Julia Siomuha, Gubin Yury), SuperStock (Biosphoto)

Library of Congress Cataloging-in-Publication Data
Names: Riggs, Kate, author.
Title: Wild Horses / Kate Riggs.
Series: Seedlings.
Includes index.
Summary: A kindergarten-level introduction to wild horses,
covering their growth process, behaviors, the wilderness they
call home, and such defining features as their manes and
tails.
Identifiers: LCCN 2016054477 / ISBN 978-1-60818-870-3
(hardcover) / ISBN 978-1-62832-485-3 (pbk) / ISBN 978-1-
56660-918-0 (eBook)

Subjects: Wild horses—Juvenile literature.
Classification: LCC SF360.R543 2017 / DDC 636.1/3—dc23

CCSS: RI.K.1, 2, 3, 4, 5, 6, 7;
RI.1.1, 2, 3, 4, 5, 6, 7; RF.K.1, 3; RF.1.1

First Edition HC 9 8 7 6 5 4 3 2 1
First Edition PBK 9 8 7 6 5 4 3 2 1

TABLE OF CONTENTS

Hello, wild horses!

Mustangs are called wild horses. So are brumbies. But these horses were trained long ago.

Przewalski's (*sheh-VAWL-skees*) horses are truly wild.

They are shorter
than other horses.
Their manes stick
up straight.

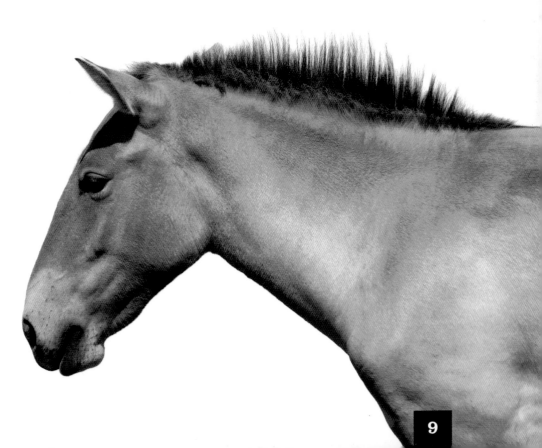

9

Mustangs are the largest wild horses.

Their manes are long. They have hair between their ears, too.

Horses eat grass.
Their big teeth chew
stems and branches.

A baby horse
is called a foal.
Foals drink milk.
Then they start
eating plants.

Bands of horses move together. They eat grass and drink water. The horses run from danger.

Goodbye,

wild horses!

Picture a Wild Horse

tail

coat

mane

ear

eye

forelock

mouth

hoof

21

Words to Know

bands: small family groups of wild horses led by a male, called a stallion

brumbies: wild horses from Australia

manes: the hair that runs down the back of a horse's neck

Read More

Olson, Bethany. *Baby Horses.*
Minneapolis: Bellwether Media, 2014.

Riggs, Kate. *Wild Horses.*
Mankato, Minn.: Creative Education, 2015.

Websites

National Geographic Kids: Przewalski's Horse
http://kids.nationalgeographic.com/animals/przewalskis
-horse/#przewalskis-horse-colt.jpg
Learn more about how these horses are protected today.

Super Coloring: Horses Coloring Pages
http://www.supercoloring.com/coloring-pages
/mammals/horses
Print out pictures of mustangs to color.

Index